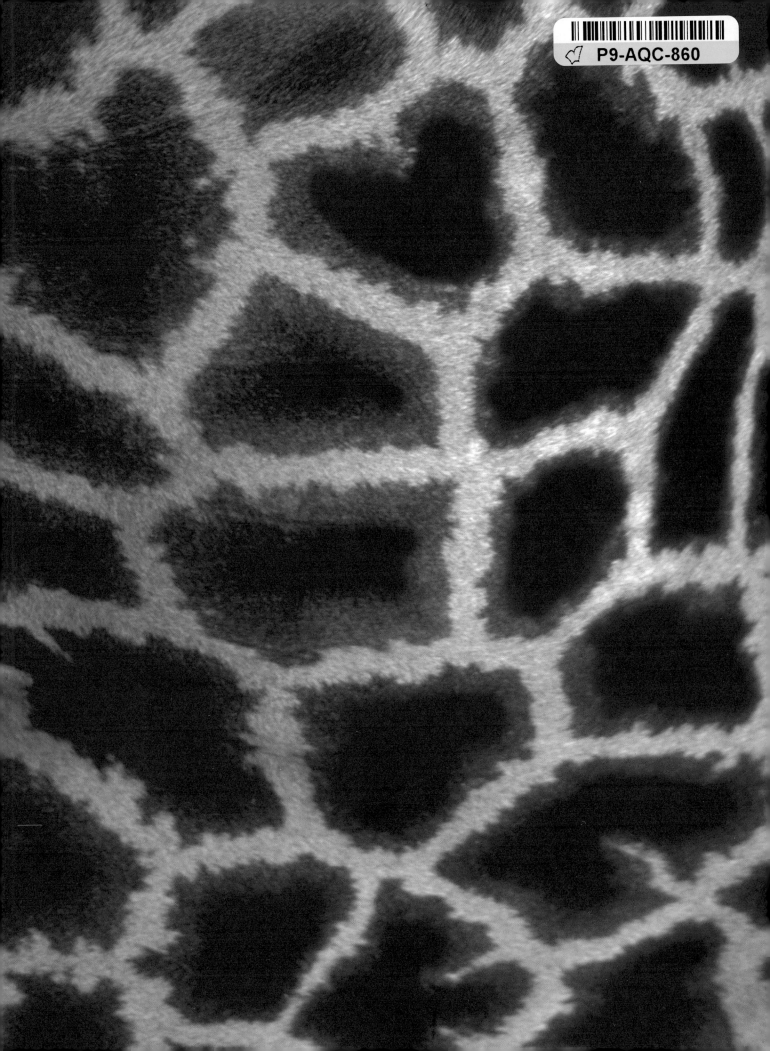

Why Am I Rare?

early bird nature books

Red Deer Press

Early Bird Nature Books are published by
Red Deer Press
813 MacKimmie Library Tower, 2500 University Drive NW
Calgary Alberta Canada T2N 1N4

Credits
Edited for the Press by Peter Carver.
Cover design by Ben Kunz, Kunz Design.
Text design by Jamie Heneghan, Liquid Silk Design.
Printed and bound in Canada by Friesens for Red Deer Press.

Acknowledgments
Financial support provided by the Alberta Foundation for the Arts, a beneficiary of the Lottery Fund of the Government of Alberta, and by the Canada Council, the Department of Canadian Heritage and the University of Calgary.

THE CANADA COUNCIL | LE CONSEIL DES ARTS
FOR THE ARTS | DU CANADA
SINCE 1957 | DEPUIS 1957

National Library of Canada Cataloguing in Publication Data
Gilders, Michelle A., 1966–
Why am I rare?
(Early bird nature books)
ISBN 0-88995-274-4
1. Endangered species—Juvenile literature. 2. Rare animals—Juvenile literature. I. Title.
II. Series: Gilders, Michelle A., 1966– Early bird nature books.
QL83.G54 2002   j591.68   C2002-910824-1

5 4 3 2 1

To Ellen Stephanie Gilders, with love

Author's Acknowledgments
Thanks to the Calgary Zoo (Calgary, Alberta), San Diego Zoo and Wild Animal Park (San Diego, California), The Living Desert (Palm Desert, California), Busch Gardens Tampa (Tampa, Florida), Jacksonville Zoo (Jacksonville, Florida), St. Augustine Alligator Farm (St. Augustine, Florida), Zoo Atlanta (Atlanta, Georgia), Gladys Porter Zoo (Brownsville, Texas), Houston Zoo (Houston, Texas), Chester Zoo (United Kingdom), Marwell Zoo (United Kingdom), Jersey Zoo (Channel Islands), Tidbinbilla Nature Reserve (Australian Capital Territory, Australia), Australian Wildlife Park (Sydney, Australia), and the Mount Bruce National Wildlife Centre (Mount Bruce, New Zealand) for allowing me to photograph their animals. Also thanks to the Royal Tyrrell Museum of Palaeontology (Drumheller, Alberta) for allowing me to photograph museum specimens. Thanks to my editor, Peter Carver, and to Dennis Johnson, Gary Stolz, PhD, (for serving as technical advisor on this and many other books), and Carrie, Richard, Harriet, and William Green for reading over some early drafts and for giving me a place to stay in Australia! My thanks also go to my parents and to Chris and Fiona. And to Ellen, who is still too young to know what an inspiration she is to me.

Contents

How Many Species Exist?

How many different types of animals and plants are there in the world?

How many kinds of birds, mammals, and other animals can you see in your own garden, or in the park, or on the grounds of your school? If you add them all up, there may be 10 or 20, depending on where you live.

How many different animals are there in a zoo? Most zoos only have a few hundred different kinds of mammals, birds, reptiles, and amphibians.

So how many different types of animals (called species) do you think there are on Earth?

Most of the world's plants and animals are found in tropical forests in places like Brazil, Indonesia, Central Africa, and Central America. These areas are very warm and they get a lot of rain.

Don't forget plants when you think about species! There are about 300,000 species of vascular plants like flowers, shrubs, and trees.

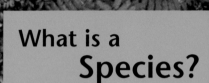

What is a Species?

A species is a group of similar animals or plants that look alike and that breed naturally with each other. Sometimes a species may be divided into one or more subspecies. Subspecies are very closely related to each other—like Bengal tigers and Siberian tigers— but because they live in different places, they do not usually breed with each other. Over millions of years of evolution, subspecies may actually become separate species.

▲ *There are nearly 10,000 species of birds. This young Whooping Crane will grow up to be the largest bird in North America.*

▼ *The Komodo dragon is just one of 6,500 species of reptiles.*

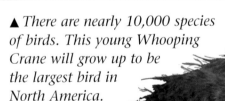

◄*Many little animals, like this pygmy marmoset from South America, live in tropical forests.*

4

▼ *The corroboree frog is a very rare amphibian from Australia. There are around 4,500 different species of amphibians.*

▼ *Newts and salamanders, like this Mandarin emperor newt, are another type of amphibian.*

We are still finding new species of mammals and birds. But it is even harder to find and count small creatures like insects, worms, or tiny microscopic animals that live in the soil and water. Some people think there are between 5 and 10 million species of plants and animals on Earth. That's a lot, but others think the number could be as high as 100 million. If you started counting now, it would take you over four months of constant counting to reach 10 million! How long do you think it will take people to find all those new species?

Every year, people travel to remote areas to search carefully for animals and plants that have never been seen before. So far, we have only named about 1.7 million species—and more than half of those are insects! If you want to discover something, become a biologist—you may have an animal or plant named after you!

◄*Of the 4,800 different types of mammals, there are about 38 species of cats, including this beautiful snow leopard. Snow leopards are found in the mountains of Central Asia. Sadly, their beautiful coats are sought after by hunters. Only about 7,300 of the cats are left.*

When is a Species Rare?

If you live in North America, you might think that penguins, koalas, and kangaroos are rare because you never see one in the wild. Some species are found all over the world—like us!—but most species are only found in a few places.

We usually call a species rare when there are only a few hundred or a few thousand of them left in the entire world. A species may be rare because its members only live on one small island or on a mountaintop.

▲ *Penguins like these King Penguins aren't really rare. It's just that they live in remote places where very few people live.*

But today, most endangered species are rare because people have killed too many of them or have destroyed the places where they live.

There is no magic number to tell us when a species is rare or threatened with extinction. Some animals breed quickly and have lots of young, while others may only have one or two young in a lifetime.

You've probably heard of the Dodo. The Dodo was a large, flightless bird (think of a huge pigeon) that lived on the island of Mauritius in the Indian Ocean. You might think the Dodo was a stupid bird that couldn't fly and was easy to catch. But in fact Dodos were very well adapted to their island home. They didn't need to fly because on their island there were no animals that ate them—until people arrived. People didn't understand that if they killed too many of the birds they could wipe them out. Today the phrase "dead as a Dodo" is used to describe something that is gone forever.

▶ *Koalas are only found in Australia.*

◀*Eastern grey kangaroos are common in Eastern Australia, but the only place you'll see them in North America is in a zoo!*

◄Even rats sometimes need protection. This animal is a Malagasy giant jumping rat. Like the Madagascar Teal (below), this rat is only found only in Madagascar.

▲ The Takahe from New Zealand is a large rail, sort of like a giant coot or moorhen. People brought animals like dogs, cats, and rats that ate the birds and their eggs. Now the Takahe is nearly extinct.

▲ New Zealand's Black Stilt is one of the rarest birds in the world. Fewer than 80 are left. Like the Takahe, the Black Stilt has fallen prey to alien predators introduced by people.

▲ The rare Madagascar Teal is only found on the island of Madagascar. Of the 250 different species of birds found on the island, 106 are found nowhere else in the world.

People kill animals for meat, fur, ivory, feathers, bones, and other parts. Animals are also killed when people try to catch them to sell as pets. Animals lose their homes when people cut forests, drain wetlands, plant crops, and build cities. When the places where animals live are destroyed, they have nowhere to go.

When people travel they often bring animals and plants with them like cats, dogs, rats, mice, rabbits, weeds or even trees that don't belong in the new place. These species compete with native species. They eat the food that native wildlife needs, and they can spread diseases.

► Hawaiian Geese, also called Nene, are only found on two of the Hawaiian islands. These birds do very well in zoos. They are still rare in the wild even though biologists have released hundreds of them. The geese are killed by dogs and cats and often struck by cars.

7

Is Extinction Natural?

Extinction is part of nature. A species is said to be extinct when no living animals or plants of that species are left. Scientists believe that the Earth has experienced five great extinctions, including the one that killed off the dinosaurs. All species eventually become extinct, but today people are driving species to extinction faster than ever before. People are causing this sixth great extinction.

If extinction is natural, you may think it doesn't matter if some species go extinct, especially when new species are being discovered every year. But we need all the species that exist. We need plants and animals for food, to clean our water, to give us medicines, and to use as fuel. Much of the oxygen we breathe comes from plants in the Amazon rainforest. Every time you take a breath of fresh air you are breathing in air made by plants half a world away!

People enjoy nature. We live in a wonderful world. It would be very sad if we no longer had pandas, tigers, or whales to look at. But don't think that we should only save animals that are cute and cuddly. Even the smallest (or ugliest!) frog or insect is important to keeping nature healthy. We should save animals from extinction simply because we can.

▲ Dinosaurs lived for millions of years before going extinct.

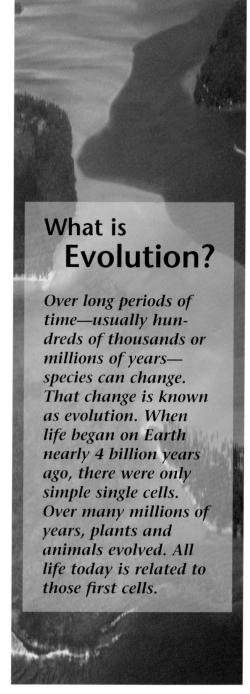

What is Evolution?

Over long periods of time—usually hundreds of thousands or millions of years—species can change. That change is known as evolution. When life began on Earth nearly 4 billion years ago, there were only simple single cells. Over many millions of years, plants and animals evolved. All life today is related to those first cells.

◄Sixty-five million years ago, an asteroid crashed into the Earth. The impact caused fires, and dust blocked out the sun. Many plants died, and soon the dinosaurs had nothing to eat.

▶ Islands often have lots of rare species. Because many islands are small, people can quickly destroy the little habitat they have. The Puerto Rican crested toad is only found on the island of Puerto Rico. It is not a pretty animal, but we should still try to save it from extinction.

Tigers

Tigers are the largest cats in the world. The largest tiger weighs as much as five grown men. Once there were eight different kinds (or subspecies) of tiger, each found in a different part of the world. Today only five subspecies of tigers survive: the Amur or Siberian tiger, Sumatran tiger, Indochinese tiger, Bengal tiger, and Chinese tiger. All are very rare, but the Chinese tiger is probably the rarest of all with less than 100 in the wild.

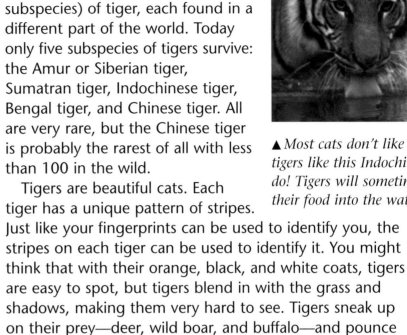

▲ *Most cats don't like water, but tigers like this Indochinese tiger do! Tigers will sometimes drag their food into the water to eat.*

Tigers are beautiful cats. Each tiger has a unique pattern of stripes. Just like your fingerprints can be used to identify you, the stripes on each tiger can be used to identify it. You might think that with their orange, black, and white coats, tigers are easy to spot, but tigers blend in with the grass and shadows, making them very hard to see. Tigers sneak up on their prey—deer, wild boar, and buffalo—and pounce on them at the last moment.

People still kill tigers for their coats and their bones. They also kill tigers out of fear. Some people think wrongly that taking ground-up tiger bones as medicine will make them as strong as a tiger.

Even if people stopped killing tigers they would still be threatened. They are losing their homes as people cut down trees and plow up grasslands to plant crops.

▲ *Sumatran tigers have short coats because it is very hot where they live.*

▲ *Amur tigers are the largest of the tigers. They may be more than twice the size of a Sumatran tiger.*

▶ *Between 2,750 and 3,650 Bengal tigers are left in the wild—mainly in India. Only about 1 in every 10,000 Bengal tigers is born white, making them very, very rare.*

Gorillas

Two species of gorillas live in Africa. The western lowland gorilla is found in West Africa and is the gorilla you see at the zoo. The other gorilla is found in Central Africa. This species is split into two subspecies: Grauer's gorillas and mountain gorillas.

Most gorillas live in lowland tropical rainforests, but mountain gorillas live high up in the mountains, where it can get quite cold.

Lowland gorillas eat a lot of fruit because it is common in their forests. Mountain gorillas eat very little fruit because it is rare where they live. Instead they eat things like wild celery, nettles, and bamboo. Gorillas do not eat meat in the wild, but they do sometimes eat insects.

Gorillas live in family groups. There are usually 5 – 10 gorillas in a family. When young male gorillas grow up they must leave their family and make one of their own.

Young male gorillas are called blackbacks, but when they are about 15 years old, the hair on their backs turns gray.

Male gorillas approach other families and try to tempt females to join them. They do this by roaring, beating their chests, and trying to look very impressive!

◄*Most gorillas have just one baby at a time. Baby gorillas don't eat solid food until they are three or four years old. Young gorillas learn what to eat by copying their mothers.*

What is a Habitat?

A habitat is the specific place where an animal or plant species lives. It includes the food, water and shelter that the species needs to survive. Types of habitats include forests, grasslands, wetlands, oceans, rivers and lakes.

▲ *Mountain gorillas have much thicker fur than lowland gorillas.*

▲ *Gorillas mainly live on the ground. Only young gorillas tend to spend much time climbing and playing in the trees. Adult gorillas are just too big to climb very high.*

▲ *Baby gorillas stay close to their mothers. When they get a bit older they will play with other young gorillas and even with the silverback.*

▶ *Gorilla families are led by a male silverback. He gets his name from the silvery hairs on his back. The silverback protects his family from predators, people and other gorillas.*

Gorillas are very intelligent. Wild gorillas don't use tools, but they do take medicine if they are feeling ill! Did you know that many of the medicines we use when we are sick come from plants? Gorillas know that eating some plants (and even clay!) makes them feel better if they have an upset stomach.

Some people hunt gorillas for food. Wildlife used as food is called bushmeat. Poachers also kill adult gorillas so they can catch the babies to sell as pets. As if all this wasn't enough, gorillas are also losing their forests to loggers and farmers. There may be as many as 100,000 western lowland gorillas in Africa, but there are just 5,000 Grauer's gorillas and 650 mountain gorillas.

▶ *Gorillas, like this lowland gorilla, are apes, just like us. Biologists call them great apes. The other great apes are orangutans, chimpanzees, and bonobos.*

11

Pandas

We all know what a giant panda looks like, even if we have never seen a live one. This rare animal from China is unlike any other type of bear. There are fewer than 1,000 giant pandas in the wild, and only a few are kept in zoos outside China.

While other bears eat meat, giant pandas feed almost completely on bamboo. Bamboo is usually easy to find where pandas live. But it is not very nourishing, and so pandas need to eat about 23 kilograms (50 pounds) of it each day.

Giant pandas live alone and only get together to breed. The tiny baby panda weighs just 90–130 grams (3– 4.5 ounces)—about the weight of a hamster. For the first few months of its life, the panda's mother looks after it in a warm, safe den. The young bear stays with its mother, learning from her, for more than two years before it goes off on its own to eventually make its own family.

▲ *Although pandas mainly live on the ground, they are very good at climbing.*

▶ *Pandas live where it snows, and their black and white coats may help to camouflage them. Sadly, some people try to kill them for their skins.*

▼ *Red pandas usually come out at night and spend the day curled up in a tree.*

▲ *Giant pandas spend up to 14 hours every day eating!*

Giant pandas once lived in many parts of southern and eastern China, but today they are only found in six small areas of forest. They have lost most of their habitat because people have cleared the forests to make way for farms and towns.

Another type of panda also lives in Asia, but it is a very different animal. The lesser or red panda is a small raccoon-like animal. There are more red pandas in the wild than giant pandas—about 2,500 adults—but that still isn't very many. Red pandas are also losing their forests as people cut the trees down, and young animals are often killed by domestic dogs.

◄*Red pandas eat bamboo, but they also eat roots and fruits. They may even eat small birds and rodents. Red pandas are very curious, but if frightened, they will hiss and snort.*

Parrots

There are hundreds of different species of parrots. Many of them are brightly colored, and in many species the males and females look alike. Parrots live in places like Africa, South and Central America, Australia, New Zealand, and Mexico.

The world's largest parrots are found in South America. Some of them have wingspans of more than 1 meter (3.2 feet).

Parrots have always been popular as pets. In the past thousands of birds were caught by people who wanted to sell them. But when the birds were shipped to other countries, many died. Now lots of countries have passed laws that ban people from catching these beautiful birds. Of the more than 350 species of parrots, nearly 100 are endangered. Lots of parrots are rare because their forests have been cut down for farms and towns.

▲ *The long-tailed Echo Parakeet is found only on the island of Mauritius in the Indian Ocean. Most of the bird's habitat has gone, and alien species, like rats and snakes, hunt the few birds that are left.*

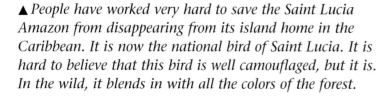

▲ *People have worked very hard to save the Saint Lucia Amazon from disappearing from its island home in the Caribbean. It is now the national bird of Saint Lucia. It is hard to believe that this bird is well camouflaged, but it is. In the wild, it blends in with all the colors of the forest.*

▶ *The Thick-billed Parrot was once hunted for food. Today, no Thick-billed Parrots are left in the United States, but 1,000 – 4,000 of them can still be found in Mexico.*

What are Indigenous Species?

Indigenous species (also known as native species) are animals or plants that are found somewhere naturally. Thick-billed Parrots are indigenous to North America. White rhinoceroses are indigenous to Africa. Rabbits are not indigenous to Australia because people took them there. Animals or plants that are not indigenous are sometimes called alien, exotic or introduced species.

▲ *The Hyacinth Macaw is one of the world's largest parrots. It eats a special kind of nut that grows on palm trees.*

To save parrots from extinction, biologists try to raise them in captivity. Sometimes, biologists will take eggs out of the nest of a very rare species and put them into the nests of similar but common species. The eggs are then hatched by foster parent birds. This lets the rare species lay more eggs, and so the biologists can raise even more of the rare parrots.

▶ *The Blue-throated Macaw is one of the rarest species of birds in the world. Only about 200 exist. They are found only in a small area of Bolivia in South America. Because Blue-throated Macaws only eat palm nuts from one species of tree, it is important that the trees are protected as well as the birds.*

◀*Fifteen years ago only 10 Echo Parakeets were left alive, and biologists worked very hard to breed them. There are now about 120 of the birds and quite a few have been released back into the wild.*

15

Alligators and Crocodiles

What makes an alligator different from a crocodile? The two may look similar, but they are quite different. Biologists tell them apart by differences in their skulls, scales, and teeth. Another difference is that alligators tend to like freshwater while crocodiles often like saltwater.

We think of alligators and crocodiles as dangerous, but most of them feed on fish, turtles, and other small animals. Only the largest crocodiles and alligators will attack animals as large as deer or zebra.

Many species of crocodiles and alligators—like the Chinese alligator, Philippine crocodile, and Cuban crocodile—are very rare now. Why? Because they have been hunted for their meat and skins, lost their ponds and rivers to development, or been killed out of fear. There may be as many as 6,000 Cuban crocodiles in the wild, but there are less than 200 adults of both the Chinese alligators and Philippine crocodiles.

It can be hard to get people to protect animals like crocodiles and alligators. Reptiles are not cute and cuddly like pandas, but crocodiles and alligators are very important predators. By helping to control the populations of other animals like rodents, deer, and fish, crocodiles and alligators keep ecosystems healthy. Conservation is not just about protecting animals we think are pretty or cuddly or intelligent.

▲ *Found only in the Philippines, this crocodile must share its home with more than 70 million people. With more people, there is less room for crocodiles.*

▶ *It was the Chinese alligator that gave rise to myths about dragons in China. It's easy to understand why!*

◄Crocodiles have longer and narrower heads than alligators. If the animal has its mouth closed and you can still see many of its teeth, then it is probably a crocodile. This is a Cuban crocodile.

▲ Crocodiles and alligators, like this Cuban crocodile, have lots of teeth, but they don't chew their prey. They use their teeth to tear off chunks of meat and then swallow it whole.

What is a Hybrid?

A hybrid results when two different species breed. For example, lions and tigers have sometimes bred in captivity, although they never do in the wild. One of the reasons that Cuban crocodiles are rare is because in the wild some of them are breeding with American crocodiles. Because hybrids are a mix of two different species, they often cannot have babies of their own.

▲ Crocodiles have been around for at least 240 million years. They even survived the asteroid that wiped out the dinosaurs! But this little Philippine crocodile will have a hard time growing up. Many animals—like birds—eat little crocodiles.

▲ The Chinese alligator is one of the world's smallest alligators. It is only about 2 meters (6.5 feet) long.

17

Elephants

Elephants are the largest land mammals in the world.

There are two types of African elephants and one type of Asiatic elephant. People used to think there was just one species of elephant in Africa, but biologists now know that there are two—one is the forest elephant that lives in dense forests in Central and West Africa, and the other is the savannah elephant that lives in the grasslands and open woodlands of Eastern and Southern Africa.

It is easy to tell African and Asiatic elephants apart. African elephants have really big ears while Asiatic elephants have much smaller ears. Asiatic elephants are also quite a bit smaller than African elephants. A male African elephant (called a bull) weighs up to 6,300 kilograms (13,880 pounds) while a bull Asiatic elephant weighs about 5,400 kilograms (11,900 pounds), which is about the same as seventy people. Male elephants always have tusks, but females often do not. Elephants use their tusks for fighting, digging, and knocking down trees to feed on leaves and bark that are out of reach. The tusks of male elephants grow all their lives. The largest tusk ever seen was 3.5 meters (11.5 feet) long and weighed more than 100 kilograms (220 pounds)—that's like a pile of fifty bags of sugar.

◀ *Asiatic elephants have been domesticated for hundreds of years. People use them to move heavy things like logs. There are about 16,000 domestic Asiatic elephants, but their numbers are falling as people use more machinery. There are probably less than 50,000 Asiatic elephants left in the wild.*

▲ *Elephants like these Asiatic elephants live in family groups, each one led by the oldest and wisest female.*

▲ *Elephants often have dust baths. The dust where this African elephant lives is red—so now the elephant is too!*

People have killed elephants for their ivory tusks for thousands of years. Because males have bigger tusks than females, hunters have killed more males than females. In some areas there are very few male elephants left. Twenty-seven million elephants once lived in Africa, but now only about 600,000 are left. That may still sound like a lot of elephants, but if people keep killing them and destroying their habitat, it won't be long before they are all gone.

Elephants are very intelligent. Elephants crossing a deep river will often walk across using their long trunk like a snorkel. People say that elephants never forget, and that is true. Elephants have very good memories and can remember where to find water or food in a place they haven't visited for many years. Elephants make lots of different sounds, but biologists have discovered that they make very low sounds—sounds that we can't even hear—to talk to each other over great distances.

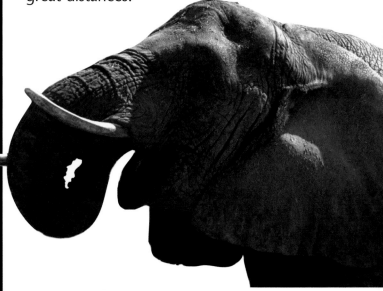

▲ *The elephant's tusks are actually teeth. Each tusk is an incisor. Do you know which of your teeth are incisors? Elephants may eat as much as 225 kilograms (500 pounds) of food a day—more than you probably eat in a year.*

Whales and Dolphins

Whales are among the largest animals ever to have lived, and the largest of all is the blue whale. Blue whales can grow to 27 meters (88.5 feet) in length—larger than any dinosaur ever discovered. Four whales placed end to end would measure more than the length of a football field. The tongue of a blue whale is the size of a car, and a small child could crawl through one of its arteries.

Blue whales may be large, but they feed on some of the ocean's smallest animals—tiny shrimplike creatures called krill. Blue whales need to eat a lot of krill! A whale might eat 3,600 kilograms (7,935 pounds) of krill in one day. Blue whales do not have teeth, so instead they use comblike baleen to filter their food from the water.

There are more than 70 known species of whales and dolphins. Biologists group whales and dolphins together and call them cetaceans. The smallest cetaceans are the dolphins and porpoises. One very rare dolphin is Hector's dolphin found only in New Zealand. Hector's dolphins hunt fish and squid, catching them with their teeth and then swallowing them whole. People are trying to save the dolphin by stopping fishing boats from putting nets in the water where the dolphins live.

Most large whales, known as great whales—like the blue whale, humpback whale and fin whale—were once hunted for their meat and blubber, and there are now far fewer of all of them. Their blubber (or fat) was boiled down to an oil that was used by people for heating. Even dolphins and porpoises have been hunted in some places.

You can see whales and dolphins close to shore in many places, including Canada, the United States, Mexico, Australia, and New Zealand. The more people learn about whales, the less likely it is that they will be hunted again.

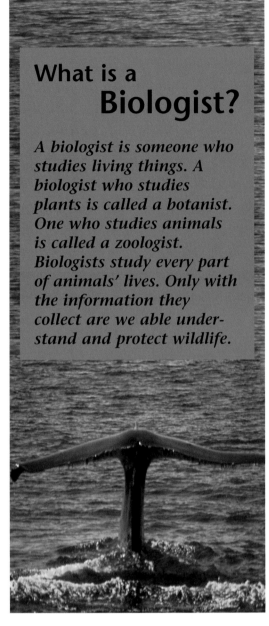

What is a Biologist?

A biologist is someone who studies living things. A biologist who studies plants is called a botanist. One who studies animals is called a zoologist. Biologists study every part of animals' lives. Only with the information they collect are we able understand and protect wildlife.

▲ *A whale's tail is called a fluke. Blue whales don't often lift their flukes out of the water when they dive.*

▶ *This blue whale has a calf with her. Baby blue whales weigh 2,700 kilograms (5,950 pounds) at birth. Your family's car or minivan probably weighs less than half that much! A fully grown blue whale weighs about the same as 30 elephants.*

◀The North Island Hector's dolphin is one of the rarest dolphins in the world. Only about 100 are left.

▼ Hector's dolphins are less than 1.5 meters (5 feet) long and weigh 50–60 kilograms (110–132 pounds).

▲ At one time there were about 200,000 blue whales in the oceans, but today there are only about 5,000 of the whales left. Blue whales have been protected from whalers since 1966.

▼ The dark fin on the dolphin's back is called a dorsal fin.

Lemurs

Lemurs are a group of primates, but they have been around much longer than apes or monkeys. Lemurs have big eyes and long tails, and most are about the size of a house cat. They have very thick, soft fur. Lemurs often live in small family groups.

There are 11 species of lemurs on the island of Madagascar, including the red-ruffed lemur, ring-tailed lemur, and gentle lemur. Another 15 species of lemurs once lived there, but they disappeared just after the first people arrived on the island 1,500 years ago.

The ring-tailed lemur has a black and white tail that it often holds up in the air, waving it like a flag. Ring-tailed lemurs use their tails to signal other lemurs in the group. A lemur that holds up its tail is easy for other lemurs to see and follow. One type of lemur even has blue eyes. It is the only other primate, other than humans, to have blue eyes.

It can be very hard to count animals in remote areas like Madagascar, so we really don't know how many lemurs are left. Biologists think there are 1,000 – 10,000 red-ruffed lemurs, 100 – 1,000 blue-eyed lemurs, 5,000 – 7,000 Lac Alaotran gentle lemurs, and perhaps as many as 100,000 ring-tailed lemurs.

Most lemurs are rare because their forests have been cleared. People also hunt them for food or catch them to sell as pets.

▲ *Gentle lemurs feed on reeds and bamboo.*

▶ *Red-ruffed lemurs live in the trees. They feed on fruits and are most active at dawn and dusk. Red-ruffed lemurs live in small groups of 5 – 16 animals. Male lemurs have scent glands on their chests, chins, and necks and can often be seen rubbing themselves on branches to mark their territories.*

What is an Endemic?

An endemic is a plant or animal found only in one particular place. Lemurs are endemic to the island of Madagascar, which means that they are found nowhere else in the world. Endemics often fall prey to introduced species.

▲ *It is easy to see where the ring-tailed lemur gets its name!*

▼ *Ring-tailed lemurs feed on fruits and leaves.*

▶ *Baby lemurs like this Lac Alaotran gentle lemur begin to ride around on their mother's back when they are about three weeks old.*

▲ *The red-ruffed lemur's very thick coat is a lovely red.*

Madagascar is a very crowded island. Lots of people live there, and they have left very little room for wildlife. If lemurs are to survive, land will have to be set aside for them, and local people will have to help protect them.

Rhinoceroses

Rhinos live in Africa and in Asia. African rhinos are big, gray animals with two horns on their heads. There are two types of rhinos in Africa—the white rhino and the black rhino—but the names aren't very helpful because both species look gray and neither of them has fur. The white rhino has a wide mouth and mainly grazes on grass. The black rhino has what is called a prehensile upper lip, almost like a little trunk, that can grasp leaves and twigs. The horns of black and white rhinos are made of a substance called keratin, which is what your hair and fingernails are made of.

People kill rhinos for their horns, which may be carved into ornaments or dagger handles. People also grind up rhino horns and take them as medicine even though it doesn't work! Only about 7,600 white rhinos and 2,400 black rhinos are left in Africa.

Three types of rhinoceroses come from Asia: the Javan rhino, Indian rhino, and Sumatran rhino. The Sumatran rhino is the most unusual of the three because it is very hairy. It is also the smallest of the rhinos and has two horns just like the African rhinos. The Indian and Javan rhinos both have a single horn. The Asiatic rhinos are the rarest of the rhinos.

▲ *Black rhinos have two horns. The front horn is always longer than the back one. People sometimes say that black rhinos have bad tempers, but they usually only charge when disturbed or frightened by something.*

▼ *There are about 2,000 Indian rhinos in the wild, like this baby rhino, but there are only 300 Sumatran and 60 Javan rhinos left.*

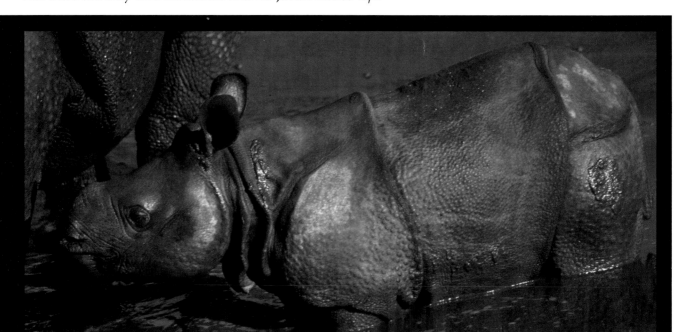

◄In some national parks in southern Africa, rangers cut the horns off rhinos to try to protect them from poachers, but rhinos like this white rhino need their horns to protect their young from predators like lions and hyenas. Young rhinos stay with their mothers for two to three years. The female will drive her youngster away just before she gives birth to her next baby.

▲ An adult white rhino may weigh more than 3,000 kilograms (6,600 pounds)—roughly the weight of three cars. The only land mammals larger than white rhinos are elephants and some hippos.

◄Asiatic rhinos like this Indian rhino look like they are wearing armor because of the folds in their skin. Asiatic rhinos have a prehensile upper lip that they use to pull leaves and twigs off shrubs and small trees.

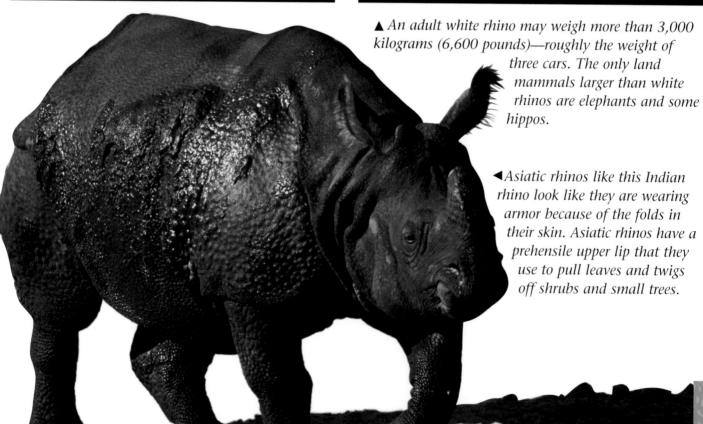

Lion Tamarins

Tamarins are tiny primates—sort of like mini-monkeys. Lion tamarins are found only in a small area of Brazil in South America known as the Atlantic Coastal Rainforest. There are four different species of lion tamarins, each named for the color of its soft fur: golden, golden-headed, black, and black-headed. Because people have lived where the tamarins are found for hundreds of years, they have now cut down most of the trees. Very few forests are left where tamarins can live.

Lion tamarins are about 20–30 centimeters (8–12 inches) long—the size of a guinea pig—and they have tails that measure 30–40 centimeters (12–16 inches) long.

Zoos have been breeding some species of lion tamarins in captivity. There are now more than 1,000 golden lion tamarins and 1,500 of the golden-headed lion tamarins in the wild and even more in captivity.

The other two tamarin species—the black and black-headed—are not doing quite as well. There are about 900 black lion tamarins in the wild, but very few in captivity. The black-headed lion tamarin was only discovered a few years ago. There are less than 300 in the wild and none in captivity.

Biologists hope to release more and more tamarins into the wild, but this will only be possible if their forests can be protected. Even though some of the forests are now protected in national parks, people still cut down the trees to use as firewood.

◄ *Tamarins live entirely in the trees and are very lively, often jumping between branches. This tamarin is a golden-headed lion tamarin.*

▲ *Golden-headed lion tamarins live in small groups, usually a male and female and their young from one or two years. Both males and females help in raising the young.*

What is an Ecosystem?

An ecosystem is a community of plants, animals, and microbes that live together in a specific environment like a grassland, forest, desert, or lake. An ecosystem includes the nonliving environment—like the air, water, rocks, and soil.

▶ *Golden lion tamarins are most active during the day, when they search the leaves for insects, snails, fruit, and even birds' eggs. Tamarins often fall prey to snakes and eagles.*

◀ *Golden lion tamarins really are golden, and they have a ruff of fur around their head just like a lion. Young tamarins stay with their parents for at least two years before heading out on their own.*

◀ *Black lion tamarins live in small groups of two or three animals. Saving animals like the black lion tamarin does not just mean breeding lots of them in zoos; it means saving the forests in which they live.*

▲ *At night, golden lion tamarins curl up and go to sleep in holes in the trunks of trees.*

27

Conservation Success Stories

Many people are working very hard to save species like the ones described in this book. If enough people help, these animals may not completely disappear. While zoos can help, the only way we can help species to avoid extinction is to protect the places where they live—their forests, rivers, lakes, grasslands, wetlands, deserts, and mountains.

There have been many conservation success stories. Gray whales, sea otters, northern elephant seals, Bald Eagles, and Brown Pelicans have all faced extinction. They were saved because enough people cared about what happened to them.

▼ *Bald Eagles were common hundreds of years ago, but by the 1960s there were only 400 pairs nesting in the United States (not including Alaska). The eagles were poisoned by pesticides and suffered from the loss of habitat.*

▲ *To help save the eagles, people raised them in captivity and then released them into protected areas. People also stopped using the pesticides that hurt the birds. There are now more than 5,700 pairs of Bald Eagles in the lower 48 states and another 30,000 eagles in Alaska.*

What is Conservation?

Conservation is the protection of the natural world. A conservationist is someone who protects the environment. Zoos can be very important in saving a species from extinction—but zoos can only hold a small number of animals. To really save a species from extinction, we must protect its natural habitat. And that is a job we can all do!

▲ *People used to hunt gray whales for their meat, oil, and baleen. They were almost hunted to extinction. When people realized how rare these whales were, they campaigned to have them protected. Now there are lots of gray whales.*

▲ *Sea otters were hunted for their thick fur. So many were killed that the species almost vanished. Sea otters are protected now, but they are still not found in all the areas where they once lived.*

◄*Northern elephant seals were hunted so much that they were thought to be extinct several different times! Luckily, a few seals escaped the hunters. Once protected, the seals recovered and there are now more than 100,000 of them!*

◄*The same pesticide that harmed Bald Eagles also threatened Brown Pelicans. The pesticides made the pelicans' eggs very brittle, and they broke easily. When the pesticide was banned, the pelicans recovered.*

29

What Can You Do to Help?

There are many things you can do to learn about wildlife and help protect animals and plants:

1   Find out what rare species live near you. You can find lots of information on the Internet and at your local library.

2   Get your class at school to adopt a rare species (pick something unusual) and learn everything you can about it.

3   Always keep your dog on its leash, and don't let it harass wildlife.

4   Keep your pet cat indoors. Cats are very good predators and are responsible for killing millions of small animals and birds every year.

5   If you find a baby animal, leave it alone. It probably has not been abandoned, and its mother may be nearby. If you find an injured animal, don't touch it—it could bite. Tell an adult and ask him or her to contact the local SPCA or animal shelter.

6   Put up birdhouses of different sizes for different species. You can even put up special houses where bats can roost and small boxes where butterflies can lay their eggs.

7   Join a local bird watching club and make a list of all the different species that you see. You can compare how your sightings change from year to year and in different seasons.

8   Don't disturb wildlife by getting too close. It is far more enjoyable to watch animals from a distance.

9   Try to reduce the amount of things you throw away and never litter (even something like an apple core is litter). If you have trash with you when you are out, take it home with you. If you see litter that someone else has dropped, pick it up. Plastic bags and glass can kill animals.

10 Recycle plastic, glass, cans, paper, and cardboard, and compost food waste.

11 Volunteer with your friends and family at your local park or wildlife refuge.

12 Join a national or international wildlife organization like the Wildlife Conservation Society or the World Wide Fund for Nature (WWF). They have excellent magazines and newsletters.

▶ Never feed wildlife—not even friendly little creatures like this Columbian ground squirrel, who is trying to make off with someone's lunch! By feeding wildlife, we make them less able to fend for themselves.

▲ Go on nature hikes with friends or family. Take field guides with you so you can identify animals and plants. It's much more fun when you can tell other people what they are seeing.

▲ When you are on holiday, don't buy things made from wildlife. Animals like this rare Indochinese box turtle are often killed and sold to tourists.

◀ Plant a wildlife garden with native flowers, trees, and shrubs to attract insects like butterflies and bees and other native animals and birds. Then enjoy watching wildlife in your own backyard.

31

Useful Web Sites

For information on wildlife and conservation visit:

The Wildlife Conservation Society
www.wcs.org

The World Wide Fund for Nature
www.panda.org

Canadian Wildlife Service
www.cws-scf.ec.gc.ca

United States Fish and Wildlife Service
www.fws.gov

Michelle Gilders
www.michellegilders.com

Information about Early Bird Nature Books
www.earlybirdnaturebooks.com
www.reddeerpress.com

▲ *A trio of Asiatic elephants turn their attention elsewhere.*

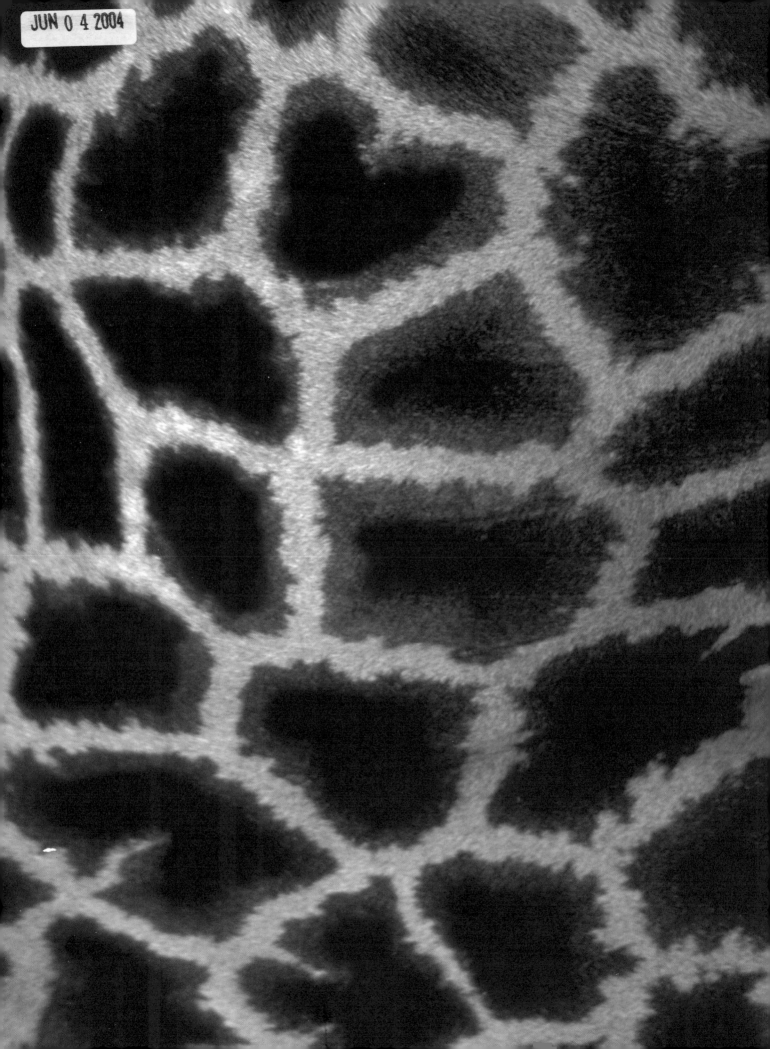

3420 Corwin Press

Sage Publications
2455 Teller Road
Thousand Oaks, CA   91320   805-499-9774
                                   800-818-7243
                          FAX 800-583-2665
                http://www.corwinpress.com
           e-mail: webmaster@sagepub.com

Publishes books and products for all learners of all ages and their educators, including subjects such as classroom management, early childhood education, guidance and counseling, higher/adult education, inclusive education, exceptional students, student assessment, as well as behavior, motivation and discipline.

Catalog

3421 Edge Enterprises

PO Box 1304
Lawrence, KS   66044   785-749-1473
                     FAX 785-749-0207
        e-mail: edgeenterprises@alltel.net
Jean B Schumaker, President
Donald D Deshler, VP
Jacqueline Schafer, Managing Editor

A research, development and publishing company addressing the needs of at-risk learners. Offers research-based instructor's manuals and videotapes for teachers and parents in the areas of learning strategies, math strategies, self advocacy, social skills, cooperative thinking strategies and community building. Catalogue available upon request. Training required associated with some products.

3422 Educators Publishing Service

PO Box 9031
Cambridge, MA   02139

                              800-435-7728
                     FAX 888-440-2665
        http://www.epsbooks.com
        e-mail: epsbooks@epsbooks.com
Dr. Mel Levine, Author

Publishes vocabulary, grammar and language arts materials for students from kindergarten through high school, and specializes in phonics and reading comprehension as well as materials for students with learning differences.

3423 Federation for Children with Special Needs

1135 Tremont Street
Boston, MA   02120   617-236-7210
                            800-331-0688
                     FAX 617-572-2094
          http://www.fcsn.org
        e-mail: fcsinfo@fcsn.org
Pat Blake, Associate Executive Director
Sara Miranda, Associate Executive Director
Rich Robison, Executive Director

Provides information to the parents of children with disabilities, their professional partners, and their communities, offering publications on school reform, inclusion, education laws, and advocacy.

3424 Free Spirit Publishing

217 Fifth Avenue N
Minneapolis, MN   55401   612-338-2068
                                 800-735-7323
                        FAX 612-337-5050
            http://www.freespirit.com
        e-mail: help4kids@freespirit.com
Judy Galbraith, Founder/President

Publishes non-fiction materials which empower young people and promote self-esteem through improved social and learning skills. Topics include self-awareness, stress management, school success, creativity, friends and family, and special needs such as gifted and talented learners and children with learning differences.

Catalog

3425 GSI Publications

PO Box 746
Dewitt, NY   13214
                              800-550-2343
                     FAX 315-446-2012
          http://www.gsi-add.com
        e-mail: addgsi@aol.com
Dr. Gordon, Author

Publishes books for parents, teachers, ADHD children and their siblings.

Newsletter

3426 Great Potential Press

PO Box 5057
Scottsdale, AZ   85261   602-954-4200
                                877-954-4200
                        FAX 602-954-0185
      http://www.giftedpsychologypress.com
            e-mail: info@giftedbooks.com
James T Webb PhD, Founder/President/Publisher

Specializes in education books for parents, teachers and educators of gifted, talented and creative children. Offers nearly forty products, including books and videos.

Catalog

3427 Guidance Channel

135 Dupont Street
Plainview, NY   11803
                              800-999-6884
                     FAX 800-262-1886
        http://www.guidancechannel.com
        e-mail: info@guidancechannel.com
Jennifer Brady, Editor

Publishes educational products, media and resources available on the Internet and through direct mail catalogs. Offers multimedia programs, videos, curricula, information handouts, therapeutic games, prevention-awareness items, play therapy resources, newsletters and other publications.

Catalog